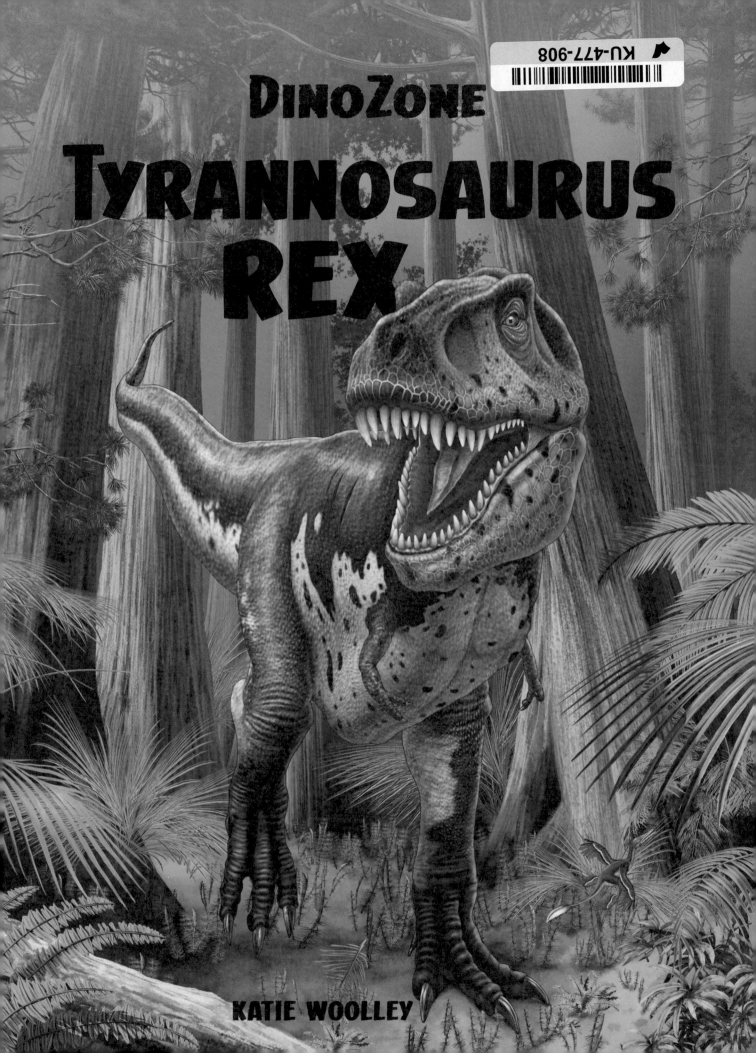

DinoZone
Tyrannosaurus Rex

KATIE WOOLLEY

This edition published in 2020 by Arcturus Publishing Limited
26/27 Bickels Yard, 151–153 Bermondsey Street,
London SE1 3HA

Author: Katie Woolley
Designers: Neal Cobourne and Emma Randall
Editors: Joe Harris and Anna Brett

Cover illustration: Rudolf Farkas
Interior illustrations: Arcturus Image Library (Stefano Azzalin: 4t, 13,
15b, 17; Martin Bustamante: 5, 6, 14, 16, 18, 23, 29; Juan Calle: 8, 11, 20,
24; Mat Edwards: 28; Rudolf Farkas: 19, 25; Colin Howard: 15t, 22) and
Shutterstock: 4l, 4c, 4r, 26-27 (Key: b-bottom, t-top, m-middle, l-left,
r-right).

ISBN 978-1-83857-258-7
CH008178NT

Supplier 33, Date 1219, Print run 9717

Printed in China

CONTENTS

What are dinosaurs?

Dinosaurs were reptiles that walked the Earth for 165 million years, long before there were any humans. We know of about 700 types of dinosaurs. But scientists think there were at least 1,500.

Tyrannosaurus rex

Triceratops

Prehistoric plant

Dinosaurs such as *Triceratops* (try-SEH-rah-tops) ate plants. The plant-eaters were hunted and eaten by meat-eaters such as *Tyrannosaurus rex* (ty-RAH-noh-sore-us rex).

Fast Facts

The scientist Richard Owen first used the word "dinosaur" in 1842. This was over 170 years ago!

Huayangosaurus
(hoy-YAN-goh-SORE-us)

Huayangosaurus's plates protected it from meat-eaters.

Dinosaur means *"terrible lizard."*

T. rex—the most famous dinosaur of all

Tyrannosaurus rex was a truly fearsome dinosaur. It had long, razor-sharp teeth and a powerful bite. Measuring 12 m (39 ft) from tip to tail, it was as long as a bus!

T. rex could be up to 6 m (20 ft) tall. That's more than three times as tall as an adult human.

Compared to its huge body, *T. rex's* arms were tiny! They were only about 1 m (3 ft) long.

Fast Facts

When: Late Cretaceous period

Food: Other dinosaurs

Size: 12 m (39 ft) long

←You!

Weight: 7,000 kg (7.7 tons)

How it moved: On two legs

Found in: Canada and United States, North America

About 30 *Tyrannosaurus rex* fossils have been found, but none are complete. Scientists think this prehistoric monster had about 200 bones. However, nobody knows exactly how many.

"T. rex" is short for *Tyrannosaurus rex*. It means **"tyrant lizard king."**

The world of T. rex

Tyrannosaurus rex roamed the Earth during the Cretaceous period, about 65 million years ago. It lived in a part of the world that is now North America.

At that time, North America was warm and humid. *T. rex* lived in forests near big rivers. It spent much of its time hunting among the trees.

Fast Facts

The Cretaceous period lasted about 79 million years. It was longer than the Triassic and Jurassic periods.

Many other dinosaurs lived alongside *T. rex*. It shared its world with other well-known dinosaurs, such as *Iguanodon*, *Ankylosaurus*, *Triceratops*, and *Maiasaura*.

Iguanodon

Ankylosaurus

9

What did T. rex look like?

T. rex had a huge, heavy head, balanced by a long, stiff tail. Its skull alone was over 1.5 m (5 ft) long. Its tail made up about half the length of its body.

T. rex was built for running quickly after its prey. Its powerful legs ended with claws that could hold down prey. Its sharp teeth were the perfect weapons for tearing into flesh!

Big, sharp teeth

Short arms

Heavy tail

Strong back legs

A human would have only been two mouthfuls for a T. rex!

Claws

Was this mighty meat-eater brown, green, or red? Was it striped or spotted? Unless a fossil of *T. rex's* skin is found, we will never know for sure. Some scientists even think that *T. rex* had feathers!

A *T. rex* with feathers might have looked like this.

Tremendous teeth

Tyrannosaurus rex's jaws contained 60 sharp teeth. Each tooth was as long as a human hand! Its bite was three times more powerful than a lion's. No other land animal has ever bitten that hard.

T. rex's jaws were 1.2 m (4 ft) long! That's the size of a 7-year-old child ...

T. rex could hack away huge chunks of meat and crush bones as it ate. It could easily tear off 230 kg (500 lb) of flesh in a single bite. That's the weight of a large pig.

Fast Facts
When one of *T. rex's* teeth broke, a new one simply grew in its place.

With its long skull and wide jaws, *T. rex* may even have swallowed small dinosaurs whole!

Hunter or scavenger?

Some scientists think that *Tyrannosaurus rex* hunted and killed most of the meat that it ate, like a lion. Others think that it mostly scavenged dead or dying dinosaurs, like a hyena.

T. rex used its good sense of smell to find food. It may have driven other predators away from their meals. They would have been scared away by the size of this mighty dinosaur.

From fossil finds, we know that *T. rex* ate horned dinosaurs, such as *Triceratops*, and duck-billed dinosaurs, such as *Maiasaura*.

Triceratops

Maiasaura

Maiasaura lived in large herds. *T. rex* probably picked off old or sick animals.

Fast Facts

When food was scarce, *T. rex* would turn on each other! *T. rex* bones have been found in the stomachs of other *T. rex*.

A fierce fighter

T. rex probably hunted alone. Its size meant that *T. rex* was big enough to take on large dinosaurs. It may have even attacked huge sauropods, such as *Alamosaurus* (AH-lah-moh-SORE-us)!

Alamosaurus

Fast Facts

T. rex was one of the dinosaurs that inspired the movie character, Godzilla!

We know from fossils that *Tyrannosaurus rex* sometimes lived together. However, we also know that these enormous reptiles often fought each other.

Many *Tyrannosaurus rex* skeletons have bite marks from the teeth of other *T. rex*. They probably fought over food, territory, or mates.

The most famous *T. rex* fossil, "Sue," has bite marks on her face from another *T. rex*.

Super senses

All dinosaurs relied on their senses to help them find food and avoid predators. *T. rex* was one of the best predators due to three of its five senses being very well developed.

T. rex often hunted at night when it was hidden from its prey by the dark. It used its super sense of smell to locate prey before attacking. We know its sense of smell was good because fossils show the area around the part of the brain responsible for smell was large.

T. rex's brain was larger than the brains of other dinosaurs that had a similar body size.

Fast Facts

We don't know about *T. rex's* sense of taste or touch, since its tongue and skin haven't survived in fossil form like its bones have.

Scientists know about *T. rex's* sense of smell, sight, and hearing by studying fossils.

T. rex's eyeballs were huge, and it is believed that they grew bigger with age. Forward-facing eyes worked together to see images and gave *T. rex* a good range of vision, unlike plant-eating dinosaurs, whose eyes were on the sides of their heads and worked separately.

By studying the ear bones of a *T. rex*, scientists know that it could hear a range of sounds. It was good at hearing low rumbles, which helped it track the movement of prey in the distance.

Young T. rex

T. rex started out as an egg, which hatched into a baby dinosaur. No fossils of *T. rex* eggs have ever been found, so we don't know what exact size or shape they would have been.

Young *T. rex* grew quickly. By the age of 14, it weighed as much as a baby elephant.

2 years old   **14 years old**   **25 years old**

It's possible that a mother *T. rex* stayed with its young when they were small and vulnerable to attack. *T. rex* mothers probably taught their young how to hunt. As they grew up, they would start hunting on their own.

Fast Facts

Some scientists think that young *T. rex* had feathers, which disappeared as it grew up.

Young T. rex

Young T. rex

Mother T. rex

How do we know about T. rex?

By looking at fossils, scientists can learn about *T. rex's* body, the way it lived, and the world around it.

The first *T. rex* fossil was discovered in 1902 by a famous fossil hunter named Barnum Brown. He dug it up it in the US state of Montana. Since then, *T. rex* fossils have been found in Canada, the United States, and Mongolia.

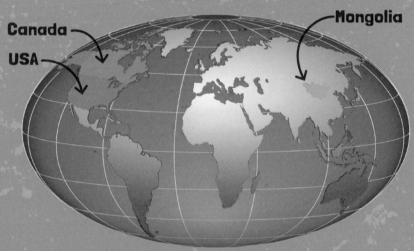

Canada
USA
Mongolia

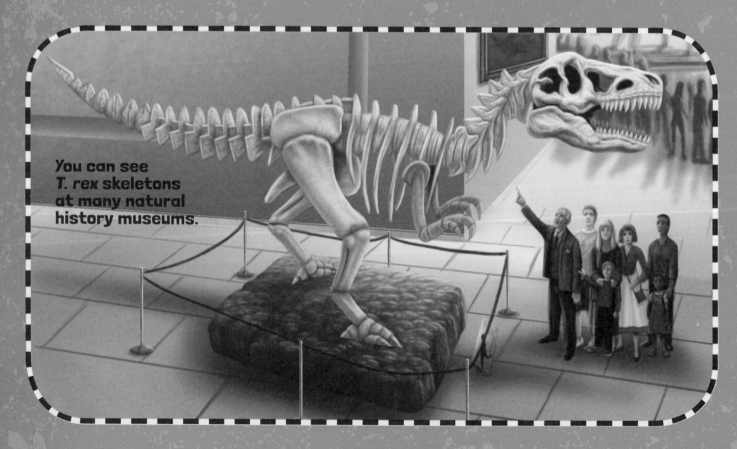

You can see *T. rex* skeletons at many natural history museums.

For a long time, people thought that *T. rex* was the biggest meat-eating dinosaur. Now, we have found fossils from some other predators, such as *Spinosaurus*, that were even bigger.

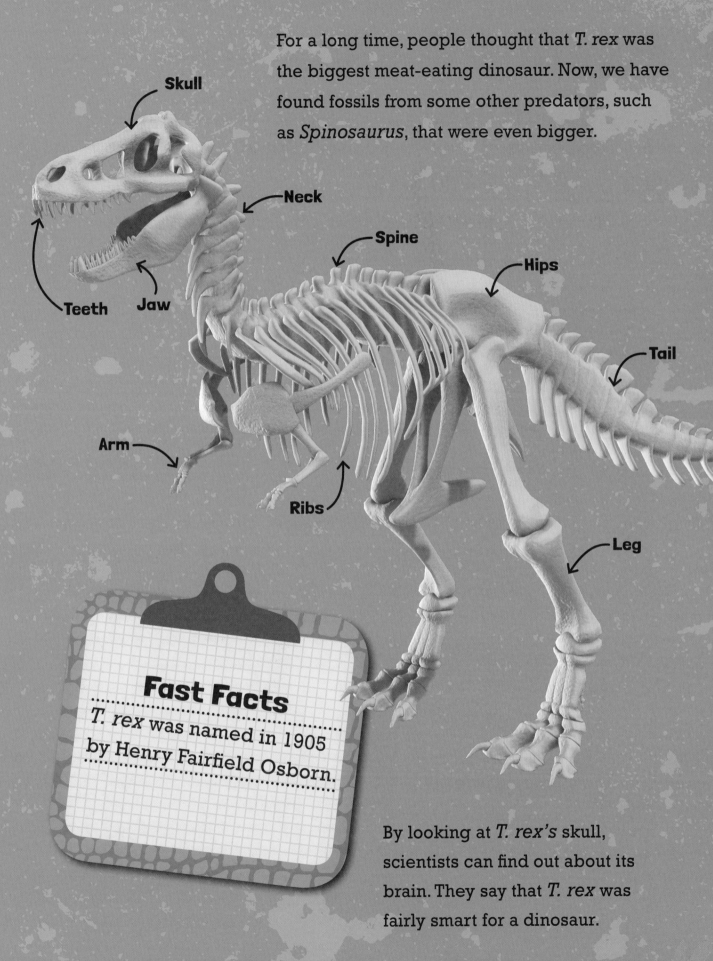

Skull

Neck

Spine

Hips

Tail

Teeth

Jaw

Arm

Ribs

Leg

Fast Facts

T. rex was named in 1905 by Henry Fairfield Osborn.

By looking at *T. rex's* skull, scientists can find out about its brain. They say that *T. rex* was fairly smart for a dinosaur.

Famous fossils

Many *T. rex* fossils have been given nicknames. The largest fossil is called "Sue." She is 12 m (39 ft) long and 3.6 m (12 ft) high.

In 2001, the most complete *T. rex* fossil was found. The bones belonged to a juvenile *T. rex*, nicknamed "Jane." At 6 m (20 ft), she is just half the length of Sue.

"Sue"

"Jane"

Fast Facts

Sue is named after Sue Hendrickson, the paleontologist who discovered her in 1990.

Sue would have been really fearsome, even for a *T. rex*! From looking at her fossil, scientists can tell that she had been in a lot of fights. Sue was about 28 years old when she died. She is the oldest *Tyrannosaurus rex* that we know about.

Might Sue have looked like this?

Sue was sold to a museum in the United States for $8 million!

T. rex's world

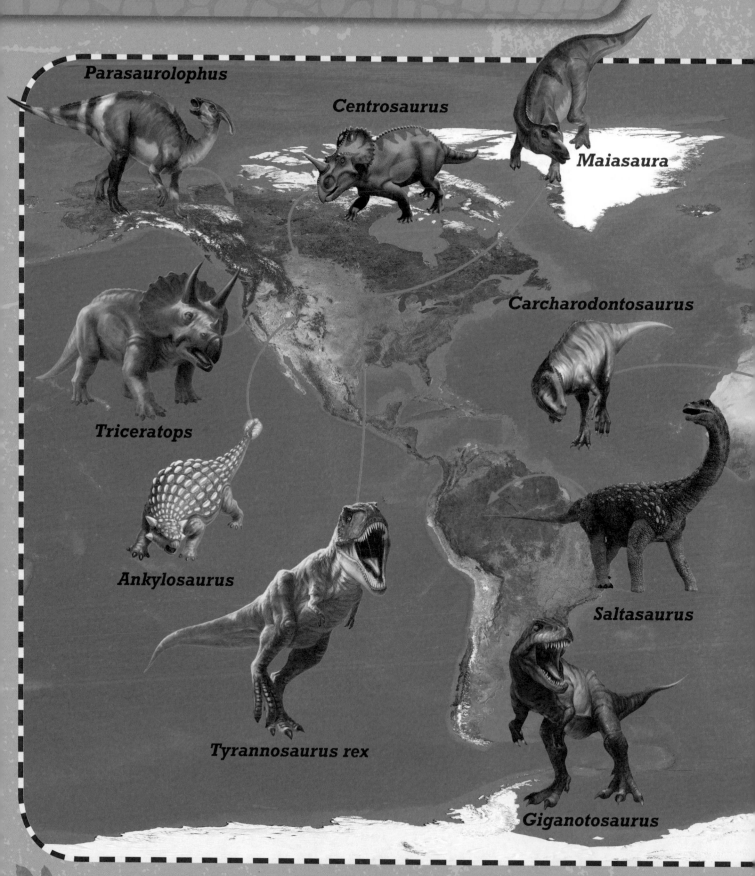

Parasaurolophus

Centrosaurus

Maiasaura

Carcharodontosaurus

Triceratops

Ankylosaurus

Saltasaurus

Tyrannosaurus rex

Giganotosaurus

Tyrannosaurs rex lived during the late Cretaceous period. Here are some dinosaurs that existed at the same time.

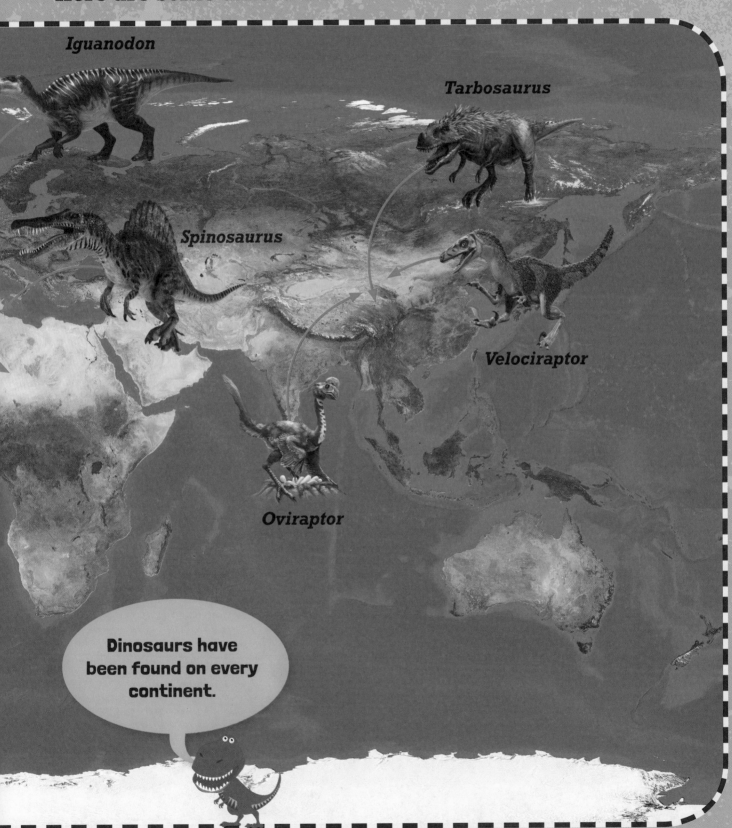

Iguanodon

Tarbosaurus

Spinosaurus

Velociraptor

Oviraptor

Dinosaurs have been found on every continent.

Myths about T. rex

There are a lot of tall tales about *T. rex*! The truth might surprise you.

T. rex lived during the Jurassic period.

False! In fact, it lived millions of years later, during the late Cretaceous period.

T. rex was the biggest meat-eating dinosaur.

False! *T. rex* was a top predator, but it wasn't the biggest meat-eating dinosaur that ever lived.

T. rex could run as fast as a car!

False! It's unlikely that *T. rex* could run at 48 km (30 mi) per hour. It was more like 19–29 km (12–18 mi) per hour.

T. rex was green.

Maybe! We don't know what its skin looked like.

T. rex was smart!

False! It was smarter than its prey ... but most dinosaurs were not very intelligent.

T. rex could only see you if you moved.

False! *T. rex* had great eyesight. It would have spotted you, even standing still!

Glossary

attack To act aggressively.

Cretaceous period A period in Earth's history, between 144 and 65 million years ago.

fierce Violent, aggressive, or ferocious.

fossil The remains or imprint of an animal or plant, preserved for millions of years, now turned to stone.

hatch To emerge from an egg.

herd A group of animals living together.

humid Having a lot of moisture in the air.

hunter An animal that searches for its prey and kills it.

Jurassic period A time in Earth's history between 206 to 144 million years ago.

juvenile A young animal, older than a baby.

mate The partner of an animal.

paleontologist A person who studies fossils.

predator An animal that eats other animals.

prey An animal that is eaten by other animals.

reptile An animal that has cold blood, lays eggs, and has skin covered with scales or hard parts.

roam To move around a large area of land.

sauropods Large, plant-eating dinosaurs with long necks and tails.

scavenger An animal that searches for and collects food.

scientist A person who studies the way that the world works.

skeleton A frame made up of all the bones in an animal's body.

territory An area of land that an animal lives within and defends.

Triassic period A period in Earth's history, between 248 and 206 million years ago.

vulnerable Open to attack, easily hurt.

weapon A tool that is used to attack.

Further information

Further reading

Dinosaurs: A Spotter's Guide by editors of Weldon Owen (Weldon Owen, 2016)

First Encyclopedia of Dinosaurs and Prehistoric Life by Sam Taplin (Usborne, 2011)

iDinosaur by Darren Naish (Carlton Kids, 2014)

The T. Rex Handbook by Julius T. Csotonyi (Applesauce Press, 2016)

What's so Special about T. rex? by Nicky Dee (Dragonfly Group Ltd, 2016)

Why Did T. Rex Have Short Arms? And Other Questions About Dinosaurs by Melissa Stewart (Sterling, 2014)

Websites

http://animals.nationalgeographic.com.au/animals/prehistoric/tyrannosaurus-rex/
National Geographic's page about *T. rex*. You can also search for other prehistoric animals.

www.nhm.ac.uk/discover/dino-directory/tyrannosaurus.html
The UK's Natural History Museum's page about *T. rex*.

www.smithsonianmag.com/science-nature/five-things-we-dont-know-about-tyrannosaurus-rex-180951072/?no-ist
An article from the Smithsonian about *T. rex*. It answers five key questions about this dinosaur.

Index